# THE FATHER IN PRIMITIVE PSYCHOLOGY

BY

## BRONISLAW MALINOWSKI

The Norton Library
W · W · NORTON & COMPANY · INC ·
NEW YORK

Books That Live
The Norton imprint on a book means that in the publisher's
estimation it is a book not for a single season but for the years.
W. W. Norton & Company, Inc.

ISBN 0 393 00332 9

PRINTED IN THE UNITED STATES OF AMERICA

2 3 4 5 6 7 8 9 0

# CONTENTS

# INTRODUCTION

*The dependence of social organization in a given society upon the ideas, beliefs, and sentiments current there is a fact of which we should never lose sight. This refers especially to savage races, where we find quite unexpected and far-fetched views about natural processes, and correspondingly extreme and one-sidedly developed forms of social organization in kinship, communal authority, and tribal constitution. In particular the views held about the function of sex and procreation, about the relative share of father and mother in the production of the child, play a considerable part in the formation of kinship ideas. The respective contributions of the male and of the female parent to the body of the offspring, as estimated in the traditional lore of a given society, form the nucleus of the system of reckoning kinship.*

# THE FATHER IN
# PRIMITIVE PSYCHOLOGY

# CHAPTER I

## KINSHIP AND DESCENT IN A MATRILINEAL SOCIETY

THE detailed study of a concrete example will show the social and psychological mechanism better than any speculations. In the Trobriand Islands [1] we find a matrilineal society, where descent,

[1] The Trobriand Islands are a coral archipelago lying to the north-east of New Guinea. The natives belong to the Papupo-Melanesian race, and in their physical appearance, mental equipment, and social organization, they show a combination of the Oceanic characteristics mixed with some features of the more backward Papuan culture from the mainland of New Guinea.

For a full general account of the Northern Massim, of whom the Trobrianders form a section, see the classical treatise of Professor C. G. Seligman, *Melanesians of British New Guinea* (Cambridge, 1910). The book also shows the relation of the Trobrianders to the other races and cultures on and around New Guinea. A short account will also be found in *Argonauts of the Western Pacific,* by the present author.

kinship, and all social relations are reckoned by the mother only, and where women have a considerable share in tribal life, in which they take the leading part in certain economic, ceremonial, and magical activities. This influences very deeply the erotic life as well as the institution of marriage.

The idea that it is solely and exclusively the mother who builds up the child's body, while the man does not in any way contribute to its production, is the most important factor of the social organization of the Trobrianders. The views about the process of procreation entertained by these natives, coupled with certain mythological and animistic beliefs—a subject with the details of which we shall subsequently become acquainted—affirm, without doubt or limitation for the native mind, that the child is of the same substance as its mother, and that between the father and the child there is no bond of union whatever.

The mother's contribution to the new

being to be born, a fact so open to observation, is clearly expressed by the natives: "The mother feeds the infant in
her body. Then, when it comes out, she
feeds it with her milk." "The mother
makes the child out of her flesh."
"Brothers and sisters are of the same
flesh, because they come of the same
mother." These and similar expressions
describe the attitude of the natives towards this, their fundamental principle of
kinship. This attitude is also to be found
embodied in a more telling manner in their
rules of descent, inheritance, succession
in rank, chieftainship, hereditary offices,
and magic—in fact, in every rule of trans-
mission according to kinship. In all these
cases, the social position is handed on in
the mother-line from a man to his sister's
children. This exclusively matrilineal conception of kinship is of paramount importance in the restrictions and regulations
of marriage and in the taboos of sexual
intercourse. The native ideas of kinship
also come to light with a dramatic sud-

denness and extreme intensity at the death of an individual. For the social rules underlying burial, lamentation, mourning, and certain very elaborate ceremonies of food distribution are based on the principle that people united by the bond of maternal kinship form a closely knit unit bound by identity of feelings, interests, and flesh; while all the others, and even those united by marriage and the father-to-children relation, stand sharply outside and have no natural share in the bereavement or grief at death.

As these natives have a well-established institution of marriage, but are quite ignorant of the man's share in the begetting of children, the "father" has for the Trobriander a purely social definition: he is the man married to the mother, who lives in the same house with her and forms part of the household. A father, in all discussions about relationship, was pointedly described to me by the natives as *Tomakava,* a "stranger," or even more correctly, an "outsider." This expression would also be frequently used in conversation when the natives argued about some point of inheritance, or tried to justify some line of behavior, or when in a quarrel the position of the father was to be belittled. I have used the word "father" so far to indicate the relationship as found in the society of the Trobriand Islanders, but it must have been clear to the reader that this word must be taken, not with the various legal, moral, and biological implications that it has for us, but in a sense entirely specific to the society with which we are dealing. It would have been best, in order to avoid introducing a real misconception, not to have used our word "father," but the native one *tama*, and to have spoken of the "*tama* relationship" instead of "fatherhood." But this would have proved too unwieldy to repay the gain in exactness, and so the reader, when he meets the word "father" in these pages, should never forget that the word must take its definition, not from the English dictionary, but from the facts of native life described in these pages. And I may add that this applies to all terms which carry special sociological implications, that is, all terms of relationship, such words as "marriage," "divorce," "betrothal," "love," "courtship," etc.

What does the word *tama* (father) express to the native? In the first place, it would be described by an intelligent informant as meaning for him the "husband of my mother." He would further proceed to say that his *tama* is the man in whose loving and protecting company he has grown up. For, since marriage is patrilocal in the Trobriands, that is to say, since the woman moves to her husband's village community and lives in his house, the father is a close companion of his children. He takes also an active part in the tender cares lavished on the infants, invariably feels and shows a deep affection for them, and later on shares in giving them instruction. The word *tama*, father, condenses, therefore, in its emotional meaning, a host of experiences of early childhood; expresses the typical sentiment between a young being and a mature man who loves him or her; while socially it describes the male person who stands in an intimate relation to the mother and who is master of the household.

So far, *tama* does not differ essentially from "father" in our sense. But as soon as the child begins to grow up and take an interest in things outside his immediate needs and the household affairs, certain complications arise and change his outlook. The child comes to know that he is not of the same clan as his *tama*, that his own totemic appellation is different and is identical with that of his mother. With this he learns that all sorts of duties, restrictions, and matters for personal pride unite him with his mother and separate him from his father. Instead, another man appears on the horizon whom the child calls *kadagu* (my mother's brother). This man may live in the same locality,

but just as often he resides in another
village. The child also learns that the
place where his *kada* (mother's brother)
resides is also his, the child's, "own village"; that there he has his property and
his other rights of citizenship; that there
are his future prospects, there reside his
natural allies and associates. He may
even be taunted in the village of his birth
with being an "outsider" (*tomakava*);
while in the village he has to call "his
own," where his mother's brother lives,
his father is a stranger and he the natural
citizen. He also sees as he grows up that
the mother's brother assumes a gradually
increasing authority over him, requiring
his services, helping him in some matters,
granting or withholding his permission to
certain actions, while the father's authority and counsel become less and less
important.

Thus the life of a Trobriander runs
under a twofold influence—a duality which
must not be imagined only as a mere surface play of custom. It enters deeply

into the existence of individual men, it produces strange complications of usage, it creates frequent tensions and difficulties, and not seldom it gives rise to violent breaks in the continuity of tribal life. For this dual influence of the paternal and matrilineal principle which enters so deeply into the framework of institutions and into the social ideas and sentiments of the natives is, in fact, not quite well adjusted in its working.

# CHAPTER II

## THE MALE AND FEMALE ORGANISM AND THE SEXUAL IMPULSE IN NATIVE BELIEF

LET us follow up the details of the natives' ideas about the nature of sexual functions. The natives have an actual practical acquaintance with the main features of human anatomy, and an extensive vocabulary for the various parts of the human body and for the internal organs. They often cut up pigs and other animals, while the custom of *post-mortem* dissection of corpses, and visits among their overseas cannibal neighbours supply them with exact knowledge of the homologies of the human and animal organism. Their physiological theories, on the other hand, are remarkably defective; there are many notable gaps in their knowledge about the functions of the most important organs, side by side with some fantastic and quaint ideas.

The Trobrianders' knowledge of sexual anatomy is, on the whole, very limited, in comparison with what they know about other parts of the human body. Considering the great interest which they take in these matters, the distinctions which they make are superficial and rough, and their terminology limited.

Their physiological views are extremely crude. The organs of sex serve for excretion and for pleasure. Their ideas about the excretive urinary processes are very inadequate. The kidneys are not associated with the production of urine. A narrow duct (*wotuna*) leads from the stomach directly to the bladder, from which it passes through the male and female genitals. Through this canal the water which we drink passes slowly till it is expelled, and on its way it becomes discoloured and sullied in the stomach by contact with excrement. For food begins to be changed into excrement in the stomach.

Their ideas about the sexual functions of the genitals are more complex and systematic, and present a sort of psycho-physiological theory. The eyes are the seat of desire and lust. They are the basis or cause (*u'ula*) of sexual passion. From the eyes, the stimulus is carried on to the brain by means of the *wotuna* (literally, tendril or creeper; in the ana-tomical context, vein, nerve, duct, or sinew). Thence, again, the desire is spread all over the body, travelling to the belly, the arms and legs, and then again concentrating in the kidneys. The kidneys are compared to the main or middle part or trunk (*tapwana*) of the system. From this, other *wotuna* (ducts) lead to the male organ. This is the tip or point (*matala,* literally, eye). Thus, when the eyes see an object of desire they "wake up," after which they communicate the im-pulse to the kidneys which, again, transmit it further. Thus the eyes are the primary motive of all sexual excitement.

The processes of sexual excitement in the female organism are quite analogical. Thus, the eyes, the kidneys, and the sexual organs are united by the same system of *wotuna* (communicating ducts). The eyes give the alarm, which again passes through the body, takes its seat in the kidneys, and produces an excitation in due course. They call both the male and female discharge by the same name (*momona* or *momola*), and they ascribe to both of them the same origin in the kidneys and the same function, that of lubricating the membrane and of increasing pleasure.

This account represents the more developed knowledge of the matter. I first obtained it from Namwana Guya'u and Piribomatu, the former a dabbling sorcerer, the latter a real expert, both intelligent men and both, in virtue of their profession, interested in human anatomy and physiology. I obtained similar statements in other parts of the island, and in the main outline, such as the sexual functions of the kidneys or of the internal organs, the great importance of the eyes and the olfactory sense, and the strict parallel between the male and female sexuality, all my informants were in agreement.

Theirs is a fairly consistent, and not altogether nonsensical, view of the psychophysiology of sexual libido. The drawing of the parallel between the two sexes is consistent. The indication of the three cardinal points of the sexual system is very characteristic of the native canons of classification. They distinguish in many subjects the three elements: the *u'ula,* the *tapwana,* and the *matala.* The metaphor is taken from the vision of a tree or a pillar or a spear: the *u'ulo,* in its literal sense the foot of the tree, the basis, the foundation, receives further the meaning of cause, origin, source of strength; the *tapwana,* the middle part of the trunk, then the trunk itself, the main body of any elongated object, the length of a rod.

The *matala,* eye, or point (as in a spear),
sometimes replaced by the word *dogina* or
*dabwana,* the tip of a tree or the top of
any high object, stands for the highest
part, or, in more abstract metaphor, the
final word, the highest expression.

In this case, the comparison is not altogether devoid of meaning, and is only
nonsensical in ascribing to the kidneys a
special function. They are regarded as a
highly important, vital part of the human
organism, partly because they are the
source of the seminal fluid, which, however, is not endowed in the minds of the
natives with any generative value. Another view ascribes the production of the
male and female discharge, not to the
kidneys, but to the bowels. The natives
also consider that something in the bowels
is the actual agent of discharge.

A very remarkable point is their entire
ignorance about any physiological rôle of
the testis. They are not aware that anything is produced in this organ, and any
leading questions as to whether the male

[25]

fluid (*momona*) has not its source there, are categorically denied.

While sexual desire (*magila kayta*) resides in the eyes, love or affection (*yobwayli*) has its seat in the intestines and in the skin of the belly and the arms, and only to a certain extent in the eyes. Hence, when we are fond of someone, such as our children, or our friends, or our parents, we like to look at them, and when this love is strong we want to hug them.

Menstruation the Trobrianders regard as a phenomenon connected with pregnancy in a vague manner, but without any special cause or function. They use simply the word blood, *buyavi,* but with a characteristic grammatical peculiarity. While ordinary bodily blood is mentioned always with the pronoun of nearest possession, which pertains to all the parts of a human body, menstruous blood is spoken of with the same possessive pronouns as are used for ornamentation and articles of apparel (second nearest possession). Thus, *buyavigu,* my blood ("part of me—blood") means bodily blood obtained through a cut or haemorrhage; *agubuyavi,* my blood ("belonging to me—blood") means menstruous blood. The women have no special way of dressing during menstruation, and there is no particular modesty on the subject between the sexes.

# CHAPTER III

## REINCARNATION AND THE WAY TO LIFE FROM THE SPIRIT WORLD

THE relation between menstruous blood and the formation of the foetus has been observed and recognized by the natives, but their ideas about it are extremely vague and uncertain. Such as they are, they are mixed up with beliefs about the incarnation of spiritual beings, and it will be best to give a conjoint account of the physiological process together with that of the spiritual agencies. Thus we shall preserve the natural sequence and perspective of the native doctrine. Since the new life, in the tradition of the Trobrianders, begins with death, we shall now have to move to the bedside of a dying man, and follow the progress of his spirit till we

[28]

trace him back to earthly existence again.[1]

The spirit after death moves to Tuma, the Island of the Dead, where he leads a pleasant existence analogous to the terrestrial life—only much happier. Into the nature of this bliss we shall have to inquire somewhat more in detail later on, for sex plays an important part in it. Here we deal with one feature only: perpetual youth, preserved by the powers of rejuvenation. Whenever the spirit (*baloma*) sees that bodily hair is covering his

[1] I have already given a short preliminary account of this subject, written in 1916, after my second expedition to New Guinea, in an article entitled "Baloma, or Spirits of the Dead," published in the *Journal of the Anthropological Institute* for 1916. But the material there contained was limited, and I was not in possession of some of the most important pieces of evidence which are here given. These I obtained on my third and last expedition, during which I had especially good opportunities of studying the spirit world through my acquaintance with Tomwaya Lakwabulo of Oburaku, a medium of very high standing. In that article I also expressed some opinions, theoretically founded, about the antiquity and universality among primitive mankind of the ignorance of fatherhood. Some of my conclusions were challenged by Professor Westermarck (*History of Human Marriage,* 5th Edition, Vol. 1) and by Professor Carveth Read (Article "Not Paternity" in the *Journal of the Anthropological Institute,* 1917). With these criticisms I shall deal in a later publication.

skin, that his skin is getting loose and wrinkled, and that his hair is turning grey, he simply sloughs his covering and appears with a new and young surface—black locks, smooth skin, and an entire absence of bodily hair. This desirable power of regaining youth was once enjoyed by the whole of humanity at a time when its ancestors lived underground and had not yet emerged on the surface. Even now we see those burrowing or creeping animals, such as crabs, snakes, and lizards, who slough off the skin and become young; while those who live in the air do not possess this power. Human beings retained this faculty for some time after their emergence to the surface of the earth, and lost it only through inadvertence and ill-will, as told in a circumstantial myth. In Tuma, the nether world, this happy privilege is still fully enjoyed by the spirits.

When a spirit becomes tired of constant rejuvenation, after he has led a long existence "underneath," as the natives call

it, he may want to come back to life again.
And then he leaps far back in age, and
becomes a small, unborn infant. Some
of my informants pointed out that in
Tuma, as here, there are plenty of sor-
cerers; that evil sorcery is frequently
practised, and can reach a spirit and make
him weak, sick, and tired of life; and that
then, and then only, will he go back to
the beginnings of existence and change into
a spirit child. To kill a spirit by black
magic or accident is quite impossible; his
end will always mean merely a new beginning.

Those rejuvenated spirits, those little
pre-incarnated babies or spirit children,
are the only source from which humanity
draws its new supplies of life. An unborn
infant somehow or other finds its way
back to the Trobriands, and there into
the womb of some woman, but always a
woman who belongs to the same clan and
sub-clan as the spirit child itself. Exactly
how it travels from Tuma to Boyowa,
how it enters the body of its mother, and

how there the physiological processes of gestation combine with the agency of the spirit—about this there are several versions of belief, not altogether consistent. The main facts, however, stand fast, and are known by everybody and firmly believed: that all the spirits have ultimately to end their life in Tuma and turn into unborn infants; that every child born in this world has come into existence (*ibubuli*) in Tuma through the metamorphosis of a spirit; that the main reason and the real cause of every birth lies in nothing else but in the spiritual action.

I shall now give an account of the details and varieties of Trobriand belief which I have collected very carefully and assiduously owing to the importance of the theme. The rejuvenation process is associated with sea-water in a general manner. In the myth, stating how humanity lost the privilege of regaining youth at will, the scene of the last rejuvenation is laid on the seashore in one of the lagoon inlets. In the first account of rebirth

which I obtained in Omarakana, it was
volunteered that the rejuvenating spirit
"goes to the beach and bathes in the salt
water." Tomwaya Lakwabulo, the Seer,
who in his trances often goes to Tuma
and has frequent intercourse with the
spirits, told me: "The *baloma* go to a
spring called *sopiwina* (literally, washing
water); it lies on the beach. There they
wash their skin with brackish water.
They become *to'ulatile* (young men)."
The final rejuvenation, or turning into the
infant state, likewise leads to the sea.
The spirits have to bathe in salt water
before they become babies again, and after
that they go into the sea and remain afloat.
They are always spoken of as floating on
seaweed, sea-scum, and the other light
drift-logs or on the leaves, boughs, dead
substances which litter the surface of the
sea. Tomwaya Lakwabulo says that they
float all the time around the shores of
Tuma, the spirit island, emitting long,
wailing sounds—*wa, wa, wa.* "At night I
hear their wailing. I ask, 'What is it?'

'O, children, the tide brings them, they come.' " The spirits in Tuma can see those pre-incarnated infants, and so can Tomwaya Lakwabulo when he descends into the spirit world. But to ordinary people they are invisible, although fishermen from the northern villages of Kaybola and Lu'ebila, when they go far out into the sea, fishing for shark, will sometimes hear the wailing sound—*wa, wa, wa*—in the sighing of the wind and the waves.

Tomwaya Lakwabulo and a number of other informants maintain that such spirit children never float far away from Tuma. They are transported to the Trobriands by the help of another spirit. Tomwaya Lakwabulo gives the following account. "A child floats on a drift log. A spirit sees it is good-looking. She takes it. She is the spirit of the mother or of the father of the pregnant woman (*nasusuma*). Then she puts it on the head, in the hair, of the pregnant woman, who suffers headache, vomits, and has an ache in the belly.

[34]

Then the child comes down into the belly, then she is really pregnant. She says: 'Already it, the child, has found me; already they (the spirits) have brought me the child.' " In this account we find two leading ideas: the active intervention of another spirit—the one who somehow conveys the child back to the Trobriands and gives it to the mother—and the motive of the insertion through the head, with which (not in this account but usually) is associated the idea of an effusion of blood, first to the head and then into the abdomen.

How exactly the transportation is accomplished is not mentioned in this account. There are natives who imagine that the older spirit carries the small baby along in some sort of receptacle—a plaited coco-nut basket or a wooden dish —or else simply in her arms. Others give the candid answer that they do not know. The essence of this version, however, lies in the fact that there is the active control of another spirit behind the baby. When the natives say that the children are "given by *baloma*," that "a *baloma* is the real cause of child-birth," they refer always to this controlling spirit, as we might call it, and not to the spirit baby itself. A feature in this controlling spirit's behaviour is that it usually appears in a dream to the woman about to be pregnant. As Motago'i, one of my best informants, volunteered: "She dreams her mother comes to her, she sees the face of her mother in a dream, she wakes up and says, 'O, there is a child for me.'"

Frequently a woman mentions to her husband who it was that inserted the baby into her. And the tradition of this spiritual god-father or god-mother is preserved. Thus, the present chief of Omarakana, the chief village of this district, knows that it was Bugwabwaga, one of the previous chiefs of Omarakana, who gave him to his mother. My best friend, Tokulubakiki, was engendered by a gift to his mother from her *kadala,* mother's brother. Tokulubakiki's wife, again, re-

ceived her eldest daughter from her
mother's spirit. Usually it is some maternal relative of the mother who bestows
the gift. Sometimes it may be the father
of the pregnant woman, as mentioned in
Tomwaya Lakwabulo's statement.

The physiological theory associated
with this belief in spirit insertion comes
more or less to this. The spirit child is
laid by the spirit on the woman's head.
Blood from her body rushes there. On
this tide of blood the baby descends gradually till it settles in the womb. The blood
helps to build up the body of the little
child—it nourishes it. That is the reason
why, when a woman becomes pregnant,
her menstruous blood stops flowing. A
woman will see that her menstruation has
stopped. She will wait one, two, three
months, and then she will know for certain that she is pregnant. Another version, but decidedly less authoritative,
maintains that the baby is inserted *per
vaginam*.

Another version of the story of reincarnation ascribes more initiative to the pre-incarnated infant. It is supposed to be able to float of its own will towards the Trobriands. There it remains, probably in company with others, floating about the coasts of the island, waiting till it can enter the body of a woman while she bathes. This view is substantiated by certain observances kept by girls in coastal villages. The spirit children are imagined to be here, as around Tuma, attached to drift logs, scum, leaves, and branches, or else to the small stones on the bottom of the sea. Whenever, through wind and tide, much debris accumulates near the shore, the girls will not enter the water for fear they might conceive. Again, in the villages on the northern coast, there is a custom of scooping water from the sea into a wooden baler, which is then left filled overnight in the hut of a woman who wishes to conceive. This is done on the chance that a spirit child might be thus caught in the baler and at night transfer itself into the

woman. But even in this case, the woman
is said to be visited in her dream by the
spirit of some deceased maternal relative,
who thus plays the part of the controlling
spirit. It is important to note that the
scooping of the water must always be done
by her brother or by her mother's brother,
that is, by a maternal kinsman. A concrete case in corroboration of these general statements was told to me. A man
from the village of Kapwani on the northern shore was asked by his sister's daughter to procure her a child. He went
several times to the beach. One evening
he heard a sound like the wailing of children. He drew water from the sea into
the baler and left it in his *Kadala's* hut
over night. She conceived a child, a girl,
who unfortunately turned out to be an
albino. But this, of course, had nothing
to do with the mode of her conception.

In this version the main difference is
that the pre-incarnated spirit child is endowed with more spontaneity. It can float
across the sea; it enters the bathing

woman *per vaginam,* or else, being placed in the hut, it enters her abdomen directly through the skin. This version I found prevalent in the northern part of the island, and especially in its coastal villages.

The nature of the spirit child, or pre-incarnated baby, is not very clearly defined in traditional folklore. Asked directly, the majority of informants answered that they did not know what it was and what it looked like. One or two, and I must add the most intelligent ones, able to give the most logical answers, said that it was simply like the foetus in the womb, which, they added, "looks like a mouse." Tomwaya Lakwabulo volunteered the statement that pre-incarnated infants look like very minute and fully-developed children, and that they sometimes are very beautiful. He had to say something, of course, since he, on his own testimony, has seen them frequently in spirit-land. Even the nomenclature is not quite definite. Usually the term *waywaya,* small child or foetus, is used, or sometimes a word *pwa-*

*pwawa,* almost synonymous with the previous one, but referring perhaps rather to the earlier stages, that is having more the meaning of foetus than of baby. But quite as often it is spoken of as child, *gwadi* (plural, *gugwadi*).

I was told, though this item I was not able to control fully, that there is some magic performed over a species of betel leaf (*kwega*) and called *Kaykatuvilena Kwega,* with the purpose of producing pregnancy. A woman in Yourawotu, a small village near Omarakana, knows this magic. Unfortunately I failed to tap this precious source of knowledge.[1]

Thus here, as everywhere, when we dissect a belief under the magnifying glass of detailed research, made over an area of a certain extension, we find a diversity of views only partially merging into a con-

[1] A statement which I guardedly gave on the authority of a trader in my article in the *Journal of the Anthropological Institute* for 1916, page 404, to the effect that there are "some stones in Sinaketa to which a woman who wants to become enciente may have recourse," I found quite incorrect, after careful inquiries on the spot.

sistent story. The divergences in this case, however, are not due wholly to geographical differences; nor can they be assigned to special social layers, for some of the inconsistencies I have found in the account of the same man. Tomwaya Lakwabulo, for instance, insisted that the children cannot travel alone, but must be carried by the controlling spirit and placed in the woman; yet he informed me that they can be heard wailing on the north shore near Kaybola. Or again, the man in Kiriwina, who told me about the spirit child's entering from the baler, spoke about an older spirit "giving" that child. In this case, as in many others, the story shows inconsistencies and seams, because it probably is the result of several mythological cycles of ideas, meeting, so to speak, and intersecting on the locus of this belief. One of these cycles contains the idea of rejuvenation, another the motive of fresh life floating on the sea towards the island, another is the conception that a new member of the family comes as a gift from some old spirit. But I cannot follow up this trend of ideas, which I merely wish to indicate—it would lead us too far into the general theory of belief.

It is important, however, that, in all the principal points the various versions and descriptions agree, overlap, and fortify one another. We have thus a composite picture, which, although blurred in some of its details, presents, from a certain distance, firm contours. The main points remain identical: all spirits rejuvenate; all children are incarnated spirits; the identity of sub-clan is preserved throughout the cycle; the real cause of child-birth is the spirit initiative from Tuma.

In all this it must be remembered, however, that the whole belief in reincarnation is not one which exercises a great influence over custom and social organization in the Trobriands, but that it is one of those doctrines which lead a quiet and passive existence in folklore, and encroach actively on social behaviour only to a small extent. Thus, for instance, although the Trobrianders firmly believe that each spirit becomes an unborn infant, and that this again becomes reincarnated into a human being, yet they do not believe that the identity of personality is preserved throughout the process. That is, no one knows whose incarnation the infant is— who he was in his previous existence.

There is no remembrance of the past life in Tuma or on the earth. If any questions are put about this to the natives, it is obvious that the whole problem appears to them unnecessary. The only rule which presides over this series of metamorphoses is the continuity of clan and sub-clan preserved throughout. There are no moral ideas of recompense or punishment embodied in their reincarnation theory, no customs or ceremonies associated with it or bearing witness to it.

# CHAPTER IV

## THE IGNORANCE OF
## PHYSIOLOGICAL PATERNITY

THUS far, we have followed the two
strands in the twisted thread of belief
about pregnancy—first of all, the ingress
from the other world of the incarnated
spirit; secondly, the physiological processes in the maternal body, the welling
up of the blood from the abdomen to
the head and down again from the head
to the womb. In this we have a theory
of the origin of human life and of child-
birth, perfectly co-ordinated and self-
sufficient, if not consistent, since dogmatic
belief never can be that. It also yields
a good theoretical basis for matriliny, for
we see, in this theory, that the whole
process of formation of the new life happens between the spirit world and the

woman's organism, and that there is no room for any sort of physical paternity.

But there comes a slight complication in these views. Another condition must be added, which is considered by the natives indispensable for conception and childbirth. And with this new condition, since it is related to sexual intercourse, the whole simplicity of the scheme is upset, the picture blurred, and we find ourselves faced by the difficult and delicate question: Are the natives really entirely ignorant of physiological fatherhood? Is it not a fact of which they are more or less aware, though it may be overlaid and distorted by mythological and animistic beliefs? Have we not here to do with a degree of knowledge empirically possessed by a backward community, but which is never formulated, for it is so obvious as not to need any expressed statement; while on the other hand, the legendary views, all the story about reincarnation, is formulated and expressed carefully, since it is the product of tradition? The facts which

I am about to adduce contain an unambiguous and decisive answer to all these questions. I shall not anticipate the conclusion, which indeed, as we shall see, will be drawn by the natives themselves.

A virgin cannot conceive.

Tradition, diffuse folklore, certain aspects of custom and customary behaviour, teach and affirm to the native this simple physiological truth. The natives have no doubt about it, and they can formulate it tersely and clearly. Let us listen to some of their statements.

This statement was volunteered by Niyova, a good informant of Oburaku. "A virgin does not conceive, because there is no way for the children to go for that woman to conceive. When the orifice is wide opened, the spirits are aware, they give the child." This is a consistent view, which, however, was preceded during the same sitting with the same informant by a detailed description of how the spirit lays the child on the woman's head. The words of Niyova, here quoted verbatim, imply, of course, an insertion *per vaginam*. Ibena, a clever old man of Kasana'i, gave me a similar explanation—in fact, it was he who first made it clear to me that virginity mechanically impedes spirit impregnation. His method of explanation was graphic. Turning a closed fist, he asked the question, "Can anything enter?" Then, opening it, "Now, of course, it is easy." "Thus it is that a *bulabola* (large orifice) conceives easily, and a *nakapatu* (small entrance, a virgin) cannot do so."

I have quoted these two statements *in extenso,* as they are very telling and characteristic, but they are not isolated. I received a great number of similar declarations, all expressing the view that the way must be open for the child, but that this need not necessarily be brought about by sexual intercourse. The point is quite clear. But, once opened up, in the normal course of events this is done by sexual intercourse—there is no need for male and female to come together in order to produce a child.

Considering that there are no virgins in the villages—for every female child begins her sexual life very early—we may wonder how the natives come to the establishment of this *conditio sine qua non*. Again, since they have advanced so far, it might appear difficult to see why they have not advanced just a little further and grasped the fertilizing virtue of seminal fluid. Nevertheless, that they have not made this advance there are many definite and telling facts to prove: quite as much as they recognize the necessity of mechanical opening up, they are ignorant of the real generative power of the sexual act. Some of these proofs are to be found in the mythological tales of mankind's beginnings on earth, and in the fantastic legends of distant lands. Indeed, it was in discussing such mythological cases, to the account of which I shall now proceed, that I was made to see this subtle, yet all-important distinction between mechanical and physiological dilation, and thus to place the native belief regarding fertilization in its proper perspective.

Mankind originated, according to native tradition, by the emergence from underground of men and women, a couple, always a brother and a sister, coming out in a given spot. According to some traditions, we see only women appearing first. Some of my commentators insisted upon this: "You see, we are so many on the earth because many women came first. Had there been many men, we would be few." Now, whether accompanied by her brother or not, the original woman is always imagined to bear children without a husband and without any other male partner. But this does not mean without the vagina being opened up. In some of the traditions this detail is mentioned explicitly. Thus, in the village of Vakuta, a mythical story about a woman ancestress of a sub-clan describes how she exposed her body to falling rain and thus mechanically lost her virginity. In the most important myth of the Trobriands a woman, called Mitigis' or Bolutukwa, mother of the mythical hero of Tudava, lives quite alone in a grotto on the seashore. One day she falls asleep in her rocky dwelling, reclining under a dripping stalactyte. The drops of water pierce her vagina, and thus deprive her of virginity. In other myths of origin the means of piercing are not mentioned, but it is often stated directly that the woman ancestress was man-less and could have, therefore, no sexual inter- course. When asked directly how it was that they bore children without having a man, the natives more or less coarsely or jestingly mentioned some means of per- foration which they could easily have used, and obviously that was all that was necessary.

Moving into another mythological di- mension—into present-day legendary dis- tances far to the north—we find the marvellous land of Kaytalugi, and in it a community without men, consisting exclusively of sexually rabid women.[1] They are so brutally profligate that their excesses kill every man thrown by chance on their shores, and even their own male children cannot attain ripeness before they are sexually done to death. In spite of that, these women are very prolific, producing plenty of children, male and female. If you ask a native how this can be, how these females become pregnant if there are no ripe men, he simply cannot understand your absurd question. These women, he will tell you, destroy their virginity by all sorts of proceedings if they cannot get hold of a man to torture to death. And they have got their own *baloma,* of course, to give them children.

These mythological cases I have adduced first, for in them our point stands out very clearly: the need of perforation, and the absence of any idea concerning the fertilizing value of the semen. But there are some convincing cases at the

[1] *Cf.* Malinowski, *Argonauts of the Western Pacific,* pp. 223, 224.

present time showing clearly how the natives believe that a girl can be with child without previous sexual intercourse, and vice versa. Thus, there are some women so ugly and repulsive that no one believes that they ever had intercourse (except, of course, the few who know better, but who are very careful to keep silent from shame). There is Tilapo'i, a woman now old, famous for her hideousness in youth. She is now blind, always was almost an idiot, and had a repulsive face and deformed body. Her unattractiveness was so notorious that she became the subject of a special swear word: *"Kwoy Tilapo'i"* ("have connection with Tilapo'i") is a form of abuse, used as mild chaff. She is altogether an infinite source, and a pivoting point, of all sorts of matrimonial and obscene jokes, all based on the assumedly impossible imputation that someone is Tilapo'i's lover or prospective husband. I was assured, over and over again, that no one ever could have had connection with her in reality; yet this woman has had a child, as the natives would triumphantly point out in an argument in which I tried to persuade them that only intercourse can produce children.

There is the case of Kurayana, a woman of Sinaketa, whom I never saw, for she is dead now, but who, I was told, was "so ugly" that any man would be "ashamed" to have intercourse with her. Notably enough, this saying implies that social shame would be a stronger prohibitive even than sexual repulsion, an assumption showing that my informant was not a bad practical psychologist. Kurayana, as thoroughly chaste in native opinion as one can be, by necessity, if not by virtue, had no less than six children, five of whom died and one of whom still survives.

All albinos, male and female, are considered unfit for sexual intercourse. There is not the slightest doubt that all the natives feel a strong disgust and horror at these unfortunate beings, a horror perfectly comprehensible after one has seen specimens of such unpigmented natives. Yet there are on record several albino women, all unmarried, each of whom brought forth a numerous progeny. "Why did they become pregnant? Is it because they copulate at night time? Or because a *baloma* has given them children?" Such was the clinching argument of one of my informants, for the first alternative appeared obviously absurd. Indeed, all this line of argument was volunteered to me in one of my early discussions of the subject, although I obtained fuller data by subsequent research. For as a means of probing into the firmness of their belief, I sometimes made myself definitely and aggressively an advocate of the truer physiological doctrine of procreation. In such arguments the natives would quote me not only the positive instances just mentioned about women who have children without having enjoyed any intercourse, but would also refer to the extremely convincing negative circumstance, that is, to the many cases in which an unmarried woman has plenty of intercourse and no children. This argument would be repeated over and over again. And also concrete, specially telling examples would be given—childless persons renowned for profligacy, women who lived with one white trader after another without having any baby.

# CHAPTER V

## WORDS AND DEEDS IN TESTIMONY

ALTHOUGH I was never afraid of using a leading question, or of eliciting the natives' point of view by contradicting it, in discussing the problems of the cause of conception I was somewhat astonished by the fierce opposition to the point of view I was advocating, which alternated with a certain lassitude and sudden, but unconvinced, giving-in. Only late in my Trobriand career did I find out that I was not the first and only person to attack this item of the natives' belief. I was preceded in this attack by the missionary teachers. I speak mainly of the coloured ones, for I am not aware what attitude was taken up by the one or two previous white heads of the mission in the Trobriands, and those of my time had only short tenures of office there and did not go into such details. But all my native informants corroborated the fact, once I had discovered it, that the doctrine and ideal of Paternity, and all that tends to strengthen it, is advocated by the coloured Christian teachers. If we consider that the dogma of God the Father and God the Son, the sacrifice of the only Son, the filial love of man to his Maker—that all this falls somewhat flat in a matrilineal society, where the relation between father and son is decreed by tribal law to be that of two strangers, where all personal unity between them is denied, and where the only duties are associated with the mother line, we cannot wonder that Paternity must be the first new truth to be inculcated by proselyting Christians. Otherwise, the idea of the Trinity would have to be translated into matrilineal terms, and we would have to speak of a God-*kadala* (mother's brother) and a God-sister's-son, and a divine *baloma* (spirit).

The missionaries are also earnestly engaged in propagating sexual morality as we conceive it, in which endeavour the idea of the sexual act as having serious consequences for family life is indispensable. The whole Christian morality, moreover, is strongly associated with the institution of a patrilineal and patriarchal family, with the father as progenitor and master of the household. In short, the religion whose dogmatic essence is based on the sacredness of the Father to Son relationship, and whose morals stand or fall with a strong patriarchal family, must obviously proceed by making the paternal relation strong and firm, by first showing that it has a natural foundation. Thus I discovered—only during my third expedition to New Guinea—that the natives had been somewhat exasperated by having preached at them what seemed to them an absurdity, and by finding me, so "unmissionary" as a rule, engaged in the same futile argument.

When I found this out, I used to express

the correct physiological view as the "talk of the missionaries," and goad the natives into commenting on it or contradicting it. In this manner I obtained some of my strongest and clearest statements, from which I shall select a few.

Motago'i, one of my most intelligent informants, in answer to a somewhat arrogantly framed affirmation that the missionaries after all are right, exclaims:—

*"Gala wala, isasopasi, yambwata*
Not   at all,   they lie,   always
*yambwata nakubukwabiya momona*
always   unmarried girls   seminal fluid
*ikasewo   litusi   gala."*
it is brimful   children theirs   not.

This in free translation means: "Not at all, the missionaries are mistaken; always unmarried girls continually have intercourse, and yet have no children."

Here, in terse and picturesque language, Motago'i expresses the view that, after all, if sexual intercourse were causally con-

nected with child production, it is the unmarried girls who should have children,
since they lead a much more intensive
sexual life than the married ones—a difficulty and puzzle which really exists, as we
shall see later on, but which our informant
exaggerates slightly, since unmarried girls
do conceive, though not nearly as frequently as anyone holding the "missionary
views" would be led to expect. Asked in
the course of the same discussion what,
then, is the cause of pregnancy: "Blood
on the head makes child. The seminal
fluid does not make the child. Spirits
bring at night time the infant, put on
women's heads—it makes blood. Then,
after two or three months, when the blood
[that is, menstruous blood] does not come
out they know: 'Oh! I am pregnant.' "

An informant in Teyava, in a similar
discussion, makes several statements, of
which I adduce the two most spontaneous
and conclusive ones. "Copulation alone
cannot produce a child. Night after night
for years girls copulate. No child comes."

In this we see again the same argument by empirical evidence that the majority of girls, in spite of their assiduous cultivation of intercourse, do not bring forth. In another statement the same informant says: "They talk that seminal fluid makes child. Lie! The spirits indeed bring [children] at night time."

These sayings are trenchant enough, as were those quoted at the beginning of this argument and in its course; but, after all, an opinion is a mere academic expression of belief, the depth and tenacity of which can be best gauged by the test of behaviour. To a South Sea native, as to a European peasant, his domestic animals, that is his pigs, are the most valued and cherished members of the household. And if his earnest and genuine conviction can be seen in anything, it will be in his care for the welfare and good quality of his animals. The South Sea natives are extremely keen to have good, strong, and healthy pigs, and pigs of good breed. The main distinction which they make in this respect is between the wild, or bush-pigs, and the tame village pigs. The village pig is considered a great delicacy, while the flesh of the bush-pig is one of the main taboos to people of rank in Kiriwina, a taboo of which they have a genuine horror and disgust. Now, they allow the female domestic pigs to wander on the outskirts of the village and in the bush, where they can pair freely with male bush-pigs. On the other hand, they castrate all the male pigs in the village in order to improve their condition. Thus, naturally, all the progeny are in reality descended from wild bush sires. Yet the natives have not got the slightest inkling of this process. When I said to one of the chiefs: "You eat the child of a bush-pig," he simply took it as a bad joke, for making fun of bush-pig eating is not considered altogether good taste by a Trobriander of birth and standing. But he did not understand at all what I really meant.

In one of the discussions on the subject,

when I asked directly how the pigs breed, the answer was: "The female pig breeds by itself," which simply meant that probably there is no *baloma* involved in the multiplication of domestic animals. When I drew parallels, and stressed the point that small pigs probably are brought by their own *balomas* they were not convinced, and it was evident that the interest in the subject, and the data supplied by tradition, did not go as far as to inspire any interest in the procreation of pigs.

Very important was a statement spontaneously volunteered to me to deny any possible assumption that pigs breed by means of intercourse. Motago'i drew my attention: "From all male pigs we cut off the testes. They copulate not. Yet the females bring forth." He ignored thus the possible misconduct of the bush-pigs. On another occasion I instanced to the natives the only couple of goats in the Archipelago, which a trader had recently imported, one male and one female. When I asked whether the female would bear any young if the male were killed, they were quite convinced: "Year after year she will breed." Thus, they have the firm conviction that if a female animal were entirely cut off from any male of the species this would by no means interfere with her fecundity.

Another crucial test is provided by the recent importation of European pigs. In honor of the first trader who brought them, the late Mick George, a truly Homeric Greek, they are called by the natives *Bulukwamiki* (Mick's pigs), and they will exchange one of them for five to ten of the native pigs. Yet when they acquire one of them they do not take the slightest precautions to make it breed with a male of the same superior race, though they could easily do so. In one instance, when they had several small pigs of European race, they castrated all the males. When reproved by a white trader, and told that by so doing they lowered the whole breed, they simply could not be made to understand, and all over the district they continue to allow their valued European pigs to mis-breed.

My article in the *Journal of the Anthropological Institute* for 1916 quoted verbatim a saying of one of my informants, which was made with reference to pigs: "They copulate, copulate, presently the female will give birth." This I obtained early in the course of my field work in the Trobriands. I commented on it in my article: "Thus here copulation appears to be the *u'ula* (cause) of pregnancy." This opinion of mine, even in its qualified form, is incorrect. As a matter of fact, during my first visit to the Trobriands, after which the article was written, I never entered more deeply into the matter of animal procreation. The concise native utterance, quoted above, cannot, in the light of subsequent fuller information, be interpreted as implying any knowledge of how pigs really breed. As it stands, it simply means that dilation is as necessary in animals as in human beings. It also implies that in this, as in many other respects, animals are not subject to the same causal relations as man, in native tradition. In man, spirits are the cause of pregnancy; in animals—it just happens as it does. Again, the Trobrianders ascribe all human ailments to sorcery, while animal disease—is just disease. Men die because of very strong evil magic; animals—just die. But it would be quite incorrect to formulate this in the statement that the natives know, in the case of animals, the natural causes of impregnation, disease, and death; while in man they obliterate this knowledge by an animistic superstructure. The true summary of native outlook is that they are so much more interested in human affairs that they construct a special tradition about all the vital concerns of man, while in animals things are taken as they come, without any attempt at explanation, but also without any insight into the real course of Nature.

Their attitude concerning their own children also bears witness to their ignorance of any causal relation between an act of sex and the ensuing pregnancy. A man whose wife has conceived during his absence will calmly and cheerfully accept the fact and the child, and he will see no reason at all in this for suspecting her of adultery. One of my informants volunteered his own case as an illustration of this, telling me that after about a year's absence he found a newly-born child at home. He told it with full conviction, and as a final proof of the truth that sexual intercourse had nothing to do with conception. And it must be remembered that no native would ever discuss any subject at all in which the slightest suspicion of his wife's infidelity could be involved. In general, no allusion is ever made to her sexual life, past or present. Pregnancy and childbirth of the wife are, on the other hand, freely discussed.

Another case refers to a native of the small island of Kitava who, after two years' absence, was quite pleased to find a few months' old baby at home, and could not in the slightest degree understand the taunts and allusions indiscreetly made by some white men about his wife's virtue. My friend Layseta, a great sailor and magician of Sinaketa, spent a long time in his later youth away in the Amphlett Islands. After his return he found two children borne by his wife one after the other during his absence. He is very fond of them and of his wife, and when I discussed the matter behind his back, suggesting that one at least of these children could not be his, my interlocutors did not understand my meaning.

Thus we see in these cases that children born in wedlock during a prolonged absence of the husband will yet be recognized by him as his own children, as standing to him in the social relation of child to father. An instructive parallel to this is supplied by cases of children born out of wedlock, where to us it would be obvious who is the physiological father, since the liaison was as exclusive as a marriage. In such a case, however, the man would not recognize the children as his, and more-

over, since for a girl it is dishonourable
to bear children before she is married, he
might refuse to marry her. I had a good
example of this kind. Gomaya, one of
my early informants, had a relation with
a girl called Ilamweria. They lived together and were going to be married.
She became pregnant and gave birth to a
girl, whereupon Gomaya abandoned her.
He was quite convinced that she had never
had any relations with another boy. So
if any question of physiological fatherhood had come at all into his mind, he
would have accepted the child as his own
and married the mother. But, in accord-
ance with the native point of view, he
simply did not inquire into the question of
fatherhood. It was enough that there was
prenuptial motherhood, which is considered reprehensible by the natives. For
Gomaya this was a sufficient reason to give
up his matrimonial plans with regard to
that particular girl.

As in the case of children born by a
married woman her husband is considered

the father ex officio, so in the case of an unmarried girl, there is "no father to the child." If you try to inquire who is the physiological father of such a baby, you simply talk nonsense to a native. The father is defined socially, and in order that there may be fatherhood there must be marriage. By one of these inconsistencies of traditional sentiment, illegitimate children, as we have said, are regarded as an improper action of the mother. Of course there is no sexual guilt associated with it, but to the native to be wrong is simply to be against custom. And it is not the custom for an unmarried girl to have babies, although it is the custom for her to have as much sexual intercourse as she likes. When you ask why it is considered bad, they will answer:

"*Pela gala tamala, gala taytala biko-po'i.*"

"Because no father his, no one man he might take in his arms."

"Because there is no father to the child,

there is no man to take it in his arms." In this locution, the correct definition of the term *tamala* is clearly expressed: it is the mother's husband, the man whose rôle and duty it is to take the child in his arms and to help her in nursing and bringing it up.

# CHAPTER VI

## FATHERLESS CHILDREN IN A MATRILINEAL SOCIETY

THIS seems a convenient place to speak about the very interesting problem of illegitimate children, or, as the natives word it, "children born by unmarried girls," "fatherless children." Several questions, no doubt, must have already obtruded themselves on the reader. Since there is so much sexual freedom, must there not be a great number of children born out of wedlock? Is this really so? If not, what means of prevention do the native possess? If yes, how do they deal with the problem, how do they regard illegitimate children?

As to the first question, whether there are many illegitimate children, it is very remarkable to note that the cases are extremely few. The girls seem to remain sterile through all their licence, beginning when they are small children and continuing till they marry; they wait till they are married and then conceive and breed sometimes quite prolifically. I express myself cautiously about the number of illegitimate children, for in most cases special difficulties obtain, even in ascertaining the fact. To have prenuptial children is, as I have said, by a remarkable inconsistency of doctrine and custom, considered reprehensible. Thus, out of delicacy for some people present, or out of family interest, or through local pride, the existence of such children is sometimes concealed. Again, these children are often adopted by some relative, and the elastic way in which kinship terms are used make it still more difficult to distinguish between actual and adopted children. If a married man says, "this is my child," it may quite easily be his wife's sister's illegitimate baby. So that an even approximate estimate can be made only in a community with which one is very well acquainted. Roughly I was able to find perhaps a dozen illegitimate children in all the cases recorded genealogically in the Trobriands. It might be put at about one per cent. In this are not included the above-mentioned illegitimate children of ugly, deformed, or albino women, none of whom happens to figure in the genealogical records made by me.

Thus we are faced with the question: Why are there so few illegitimate children? Here, again, I can speak only in a tentative manner, and I feel that my information is perhaps not quite as full on this point as it could be, had I concentrated more attention on it. One thing I can say with complete confidence, namely, that no preventive means of any description are known, or the slightest idea of them entertained. This, of course, is quite natural. Since the procreative power of the act is not known, since the seminal fluid is considered innocuous, indeed a beneficent ingredient, there is no reason why they should interfere with its free arrival into the parts which it is meant to lubricate. Indeed, any suggestion of neo-Malthusian appliances makes the natives shudder or laugh, according to mood or temperament. They never practise *coitus interruptus,* and still less have any notion about chemical or mechanical preventives.

But though I am quite certain about the absence of any means of prevention, I cannot speak with the same conviction about abortion, though probably it is not practised to any large extent. I may say at once that the natives, when discussing these matters, feel neither fear nor constraint, so there can be no question of any difficulties in finding out the state of affairs through their reticence or concealment. My informants told me that there exists some magic to bring about a premature birth, but I was not able either to obtain information about concrete cases in which it was performed, or to find out any spells or rites. Some of the herbs used in this magic were mentioned to me, but

I am certain that none of them possess any physiological properties. Abortion by mechanical means seems, in fine, the only effective way used to check the increase of population, and there is no doubt that even this is not used on a large scale.

So the problem remains. Can there be any physiological law which makes conception less likely when women begin their sexual activity early in life, lead it indefatigably, and mix their lovers freely? This, of course, cannot be answered here, as it is a purely biological question, but some such solution of the difficulty seems to be the only way out of it, unless I have missed some very important ethnological clue. I am, as I said, by no means confident of my researches being final in this matter.

It is amusing to find that the average white resident or visitor to the Trobriands is deeply interested in this subject, and in this subject only, of all ethnological questions. There is a prevalent belief among the white citizens of east New Guinea that the Trobrianders are in possession of some powerful and mysterious means of prevention or abortion. This belief is no doubt justified by the remarkable and puzzling facts which we have just been discussing. It is enhanced by insufficient knowledge, and the tendency towards exaggeration and sensationalizing so characteristic of the crude mind. Of insufficient observation I had several examples, for every white man with whom I spoke on the subject would start with the dogmatic assertion that unmarried girls among the Trobrianders never have children, that is, barring those who live with white traders, whereas, as we have seen, cases of children of unmarried girls are on record. Equally incorrect and fantastic is, of course, the belief in the mysterious contraceptives which not even the oldest residents, who are firmly convinced of their existence, have been able to discover. This seems to be an example of the well-known fact that a higher race in contact with a lower one has a tendency to credit the members of the latter with mysterious demoniacal powers.

Returning now to the question which started us on this digression, that of prevention and abortion, let us note one more point about the disapproval of "fatherless children." Here we find among the Trobrianders a certain tendency of public opinion, almost a moral rule. This moral conviction we, in our own society, share very emphatically with the Trobrianders. And with us we connect the disapproval of illegitimate children with our strong moral condemnation of unchastity. In theory, at least, if not in practice, we condemn the fruits of sexual immorality because of the cause and not because of the consequence. Our syllogism runs thus: "All intercourse out of wedlock is bad; pregnancy is caused by intercourse; hence all unmarried pregnant girls are bad." Thus, when we find in another society the last term of the syllogism endorsed, we jump to the conclusion that the other terms also obtain, especially the middle one. That is, we assume that the natives know of physiological paternity. We know, however, that in the Trobriands the first term is not fulfilled, for intercourse out of wedlock is quite free from censure, unless it offends the special taboos of exogamy and incest. Therefore the middle term cannot serve as connecting link, and the fulfilment of the conclusion, that is, the condemnation of illegitimacy, declares nothing about their knowledge of fatherhood. I have expatiated on this somewhat subtle point, because it is a characteristic example of how difficult it is to cast away our own narrow modes of thinking and feeling, and our own rigid structures of social and moral prejudice. Although I myself should have been on my guard against such traps, and though at that time I was already acquainted with the Trobrianders and their ways of thinking, yet on realizing the disapproval of children out of wedlock, I went through all this false reasoning before the still fuller acquaintance with facts forced me to correct it.

While speaking of the censure of fecundity in unmarried girls, it may be well to mention the disapproval of sterility in married women. The term *nakarige* (*na* —female prefix, *karige*—to die) is used of a sterile woman or female pig. It is a condition bad, unfortunate, and regrettable, though not one which brings shame and discredit on the person concerned. It does not entail any inferiority in the social status of such a woman. The oldest wife of To'uluwa, named Bokuyoba, has no children, yet she is the first in status, as is due to her age. Nor is the word *nakarige* considered to be indelicate, and a sterile woman will use it when speaking of herself, as will others in her presence. Fertility in married women is, on the other hand, considered a good thing. It affects primarily her maternal kinsmen, and is a matter of important concern to them, as already mentioned.

"The kinsmen rejoice, for their bodies become stronger when one of their sisters or nieces has plenty of children." In this expression we find the interesting conception of collective clan unity, of the members being not only of the same flesh, but almost forming one body.

Returning again to the main trend of our argument, I wish to point out that the scorn and disapproval levelled against illegitimacy is highly significant sociologically. Let us realize once more the interesting and strange constellation of facts: physical fatherhood is unknown; yet fatherhood in a social sense is considered necessary and the "fatherless child" is regarded as something anomalous, contrary to the normal course of events, hence reprehensible. What does this mean? Public opinion, based on tradition and custom, declares that a woman must not become a mother before she marries, though she may enjoy as much sexual liberty as she likes within the licit limits. This means that a woman, in order to have her motherhood socially approved of, needs a man, a defender and provider of economic necessities. She has one natural

master and protector in her brother, but
he is not sufficient to look after her in all
the matters where she needs a guardian.
According to native ideas, a woman who
is pregnant must at a certain stage abstain
from all intercourse and "turn her mind
away from men." She needs then a man
who will take over all sexual rights in regard to her, abstain even from exercising
his own privileges from a certain moment,
and guard her from any interference as
well as watch her behaviour. All this the
brother cannot do, for, owing to the strict
brother-sister taboo, he must scrupulously
avoid even the thought of anything which
is concerned with his sister's sex. Again,
there is the need for a man to keep guard
over her during childbirth, and "to re-
ceive the child into his arms," as the natives put it. Later on, this man has also
the duty of sharing in all the tender cares
bestowed on the child. Only when the
child grows up into a man or woman does
he relinquish the greater part of his au-

thority and hand it over to his wife's brother.

In all this the rôle of the husband is strictly laid down by custom and is considered indispensable. A woman with a child and no husband is therefore, in the eyes of tradition, an incomplete and anomalous group. The disapproval of an illegitimate child and of its mother is, then, a particular instance of the general disapproval of everything which goes against custom, against the normal course of things, of everything which runs counter to the traditional pattern and the customary arrangements of the tribe. The family, consisting of husband, wife, and children, is the standard set down by tribal law, which also prescribes to every member a rigidly defined part to play. It is therefore not right that one of the members of this group should be missing.

Thus, though the natives are ignorant of any physiological need of a male in the constitution of the family, they regard him as indispensable socially. This is very important. Paternity, unknown in the full biological meaning so familiar to us, is yet maintained by a social dogma which declares: "Every family must have a father; a woman must marry before she may have children; there must be a male to every household."

The institution of the individual family is thus based on a strong feeling of its necessity, quite compatible with an absolute lack of knowledge of its biological foundations. The sociological rôle of the father is established and defined before there is any recognition of his physiological need.

# CHAPTER VII

## THE SINGULAR CLAIMS OF SOCIOLOGICAL PATERNITY

THE interesting duality between matrilineal and patriarchal influences among the Trobrianders, represented by the mother's brother and the father respectively, is one of the leit-motivs of the first chapter of their tribal life. Here we have come to the very core of the problem, for we see how there are, within the Trobriander's social milieu, with its rigid brother-sister taboo and its ignorance of physical fatherhood, two natural spheres of influence to be exercised over a woman by a man. The one domain is that of sex, from which the brother is absolutely debarred and where the husband's influence is paramount. The other is that in which the natural interests of blood relationship can be safeguarded properly only by one who is of the same blood. This is the sphere of the woman's brother.

By his inability to touch, or to approach even as a distant spectator, the principal theme in her life—her sex—a wide breach is left in the system of matriliny. Through this breach the husband enters into the closed circle of family and household, and once there makes himself thoroughly at home. To his children he becomes bound by the strongest ties of personal attachment, over his wife he assumes exclusive sexual right, and shares with her the greatest part of the domestic and economic concerns.

On the apparently unpropitious basis of strict matriliny, with its denial of any paternal bond through procreation, and its declaration of the father's extraneousness to his progeny, there spring up certain beliefs, ideas, and customary rules, which smuggle extreme patrilineal principles into the stronghold of mother-right.

One of these ideas is of the kind which figures so largely in the sensational amateur records of savage life and strikes us at first as savage indeed, so lop-sided, distorted, and quaint does it appear. I refer to the idea held about similarity between parents and offspring. That this is a favourite topic of nursery gossip, even in civilized communities, needs no special comment. In a matrilineal society, as in the Trobriands, where all maternal relatives are considered to be of the "same body," and the father to be a "stranger," we would naturally expect and have no doubt that the facial and bodily similarity would be traced to the mother's family alone. The contrary is the case, and this is affirmed with an extremely strong social emphasis. Not only is it a household dogma, so to speak, that a child never resembles its mother, any of its brothers or sisters, or any of its maternal kinsmen, but it is extremely bad form and a great offence to hint at any such similarity. To resemble one's father, on the other hand, is a natural, right, and proper thing for a man or woman to do.

I was introduced to this rule of *savoir vivre* in the usual way by making a *faux pas*. One of my bodyguard in Omarakana, named Moradeda, was endowed with a peculiar cast of features which had struck me at first sight and fascinated me, for it had a strange similarity to the Australian aboriginal type, wavy hair, broad face, low forehead, extremely broad nose with a squashed-in bridge, wide mouth with protruding lips, and a prognathous chin. One day I was struck by the appearance of an exact counterpart to Moradeda, and asked his name and whereabouts. When I was told that he was my friend's elder brother, living in a distant village, I exclaimed: "Ah, truly! I asked about you because your face is alike—alike to that of Moradeda." There came such a hush over all the assembly that I noticed it at once. The man turned round and left us, while part of the company present, after looking away in a manner half-embarrassed, half-offended, soon dispersed. I was then told by my confidential informants that I had committed a breach of custom, that I had perpetrated what is called *"taputaki migila,"* a technical expression referring only to this act, which might be translated: "to-defile-by-comparing-to-a-kinsman-his-face." What astonished me in this discussion was, that in spite of the striking resemblance between the two brothers, my informants refused to admit it. In fact, they treated the question as if no one could possibly ever resemble his brother, or, for the matter of that, any maternal kinsman. I made my informants quite angry and displeased with me by arguing the point.

This incident taught me never to hint at such a resemblance in the presence of the people concerned. But I thrashed the matter out well with many natives in subsequent general conversations. I found that every one in the Trobriands will, in the teeth of all the evidence, deny stoutly that similarity can exist betwen matrilineal kinsmen. You simply irritate and insult a Trobriander if you point to striking instances, exactly as you irritate your next-door neighbour in our own society if you bring before him a glaring truth which contradicts some of his cherished opinions, political, religious, or moral, or which, still worse, runs counter to his personal interests.

The Trobrianders maintain that the mention of such similarity can only be made as an insult to a man. It is, in fact, a technical phrase of serious bad language to say *"Migim lumuta,"* "Thy face thy sister's," which, by the way, is the worst combination of kinship similarity. This expression is considered quite as bad as to say "have intercourse with your sister." But, according to a Trobriander, no sane and decent man can possibly entertain in a sober dispassionate mood such an outrageous thought as that anyone should in the slightest degree resemble his sister.

Still more remarkable is the counterpart to this social dogma, namely, that every child resembles its father. Such similarity is always assumed and affirmed to exist. Where it is really found, even to a small degree, constant attention is drawn to it as to a thing which is nice, good, and right. It was often pointed out to me how strongly one or the other of the sons of To'uluwa, the chief of Omarakana, resembled his father. Especially the five favourite sons of his and of Kadamwasila were each said to be exactly like his father. When I pointed out that this similarity to the father implied similarity among each other, such a heresy was indignantly repudiated. There are also definite customs which embody this dogma of patrilineal similarity. Thus, after a man's death, his kinsmen and friends will come from time to time to visit his children in order to "see his face in theirs." They will give them presents and sit looking at them and wailing. This is said to soothe their insides because of having seen once more the likeness of the dead.

How do the natives reconcile the inconsistency of this dogma with the matrilineal system? When asked directly, they will say: "Yes, maternal kinsmen are the same flesh, but similar faces they have not." When you inquire again why it is that people resemble their father, who is a stranger and has nothing to do with the formation of their body, they have a definite answer to give, for there exists a stereotyped doctrine on the subject. "It coagulates the face of the child; for alway he lies with her, they sit together." The expression *kuli*, to coagulate, to mould, was used over and over again in the answers which I received. This statement is a socially fixed view, concerning the influence of the father over the physique of the child, and not merely the personal opinion of my informants. One of my informants explained it to me more exactly, turning to me his open hand, palm upwards. "Put some soft mash (*sesa*) on it, and it will mould like the hand. In the same manner, the husband remains with the woman and the child is moulded." Another man told me: "Always we give food from our hand to the child to eat, we give fruit and dainties, we give betel nut. This makes the child as it is."

I discussed with my informants the existence of half-castes, children of white traders married to native women. I pointed out to them that some look much more like natives than like Europeans. This they again simply denied, maintaining stoutly that all these children have white man's faces, and giving it as another proof of their doctrine. There was no way of shaking their conviction, or of diminishing their dislike of the idea that any one can resemble his mother or her people, an idea condemned by the tradition and the good manners of the tribe.

Thus we see here how an artificial physical link between father and child has been introduced, and how, on one important point it has overshadowed the matrilineal bond. For physical resemblance is a very strong emotional tie between two people, and its strength is hardly reduced by its being ascribed, not to a physiological, but to a sociological cause—that of continued association between husband and wife.

The somewhat grotesque and fantastic beliefs and ideas here outlined may appear at first irrelevant—mere items for the satisfaction of the curiosity that makes a certain type of Ethnology an amusing but sterile pursuit. But if these beliefs as to procreation and reincarnation be studied in their bearing upon the organization of kinship, their importance becomes patent. My firm conviction is that the ignorance of paternity is an original feature of primitive psychology, and that in all speculations about the origins of Marriage and the Evolution of Sexual Customs, we must bear in mind this fundamental ignorance.